For Suzanne

From Nancy Haverman

To Pat and "Baby"   Aug. 1968

Love Is a Special Way of Feeling

JOAN WALSH ANGLUND

Love

Is

a

Special

Way

of

Feeling

HARCOURT, BRACE & WORLD, INC., NEW YORK

BY JOAN WALSH ANGLUND

A Friend Is Someone Who Likes You

The Brave Cowboy

Look Out the Window

Love Is a Special Way of Feeling

In a Pumpkin Shell

Cowboy and His Friend

Christmas Is a Time of Giving

Nibble Nibble Mousekin

Spring Is a New Beginning

Cowboy's Secret Life

The Joan Walsh Anglund Sampler

A Pocketful of Proverbs

*Library of Congress Catalog Card Number: 60-6224
Printed in the United States of America*

with love,
for
margaret
julian
helen

Love is a special way of feeling. . . .

It is the safe way we feel
when we sit on our mother's
lap with her arms around us
tight and close.

It is the good way we feel
when we talk to someone
and they want to listen
and don't tell us to go away
and be quiet.

It is the happy way we
feel when we save a
bird that has been hurt . . .

or feed a lost cat . . .

or calm a frightened colt.

Love is found in unexpected places. . . .
It is there in the quiet moment
when we first discover
a beautiful thing . . .
when we watch a bird
soar high against
a pale blue sky . . .

when we see a lovely flower
that no one else has noticed . . .

when we find a place
that shelters us and is
all our very own.

Love starts in little ways. . . .
It may begin the day
we first share our
thoughts with someone else . . .

or help someone who needs us. . . .

Or, sometimes, it begins
because, even without words,
we understand how someone feels.

Love comes quietly . . .
but you know when it is there,
because, suddenly . . .
you are not alone any more . . .
and there is no sadness
inside you.

Love is a happy feeling
that stays inside your heart
for the rest of your life.

CHEER UP!

Winnie the Pooh thanks his friends Don Ferguson, J.J. Smith-Moore, Sparky Moore, and H.R. Russell for helping to make this book.

WINNIE *the* POOH
friends forever
CHEER UP!

Whenever you are feeling blue . . .

It makes me feel the same way, too.

Whenever you begin to cry . . .

There's a teardrop in my eye.

When your smile is
upside-down . . .

My face also wears a frown.

So as you now come to the end . . .

Of this small book sent by a friend . . .

If you're smiling, then it's true . . .

I am smiling just like you!

This cheer-up message comes from two:
Me, of course, and Winnie the Pooh!